LEARNING TO
WALK
THE
UNFORGETTABLE
JOURNEY

LEARNING TO WALK
THE UNFORGETTABLE JOURNEY

Inspirations of Faith

TALICIA L. SMITH

Learning to Walk the Unforgettable Journey
Copyright © 2021 by Talicia L. Smith. All rights reserved.

No part of this publication may be reproduced, stored in a retrieval system or transmitted in any way by any means, electronic, mechanical, photocopy, recording or otherwise without the prior permission of the author except as provided by USA copyright law.

The opinions expressed by the author are not necessarily those of URLink Print and Media.

1603 Capitol Ave., Suite 310 Cheyenne, Wyoming USA 82001
1-888-980-6523 | admin@urlinkpublishing.com

URLink Print and Media is committed to excellence in the publishing industry.

Book design copyright © 2021 by URLink Print and Media. All rights reserved.

Published in the United States of America

Library of Congress Control Number: 2020924281
ISBN 978-1-64753-581-0 (Paperback)
ISBN 978-1-64753-582-7 (Hardback)
ISBN 978-1-64753-583-4 (Digital)

15.07.20

CONTENTS

Chapter I   A JOURNEY WITH THE KING 7
- Why Jesus? 9
- My Immeasurable Impossible God 10
- Who can Compare to you 12
- Father, Spirit, and Son 13
- The Only One 14
- Amazement 15
- The Great Exchange 17
- Who is God? 18
- Grace & Mercy 19
- The Reigning Gift 20

Chapter II   A WALK IN FAITH 21
- Faith vs. Fact 23
- More 25
- Yet, There is Still More 26
- Unemployment 27
- Sought and Blessed 28
- All I Need 30
- Expectation 31
- Time to Dance 32

Chapter III   AVENUES OF THE HEART 33
- The Love of the Father 35
- Love 36
- You 37
- Woman 38
- The Child's Keeper 39

She Has Everything 40
Marriage Lesson 42
Battle of the Heart 44
I Still Have My Smile! 45
Distress 46
Call and Response 47
My Refuge 48
Birthday Poem 49
Residue 50

Chapter IV   COMING OUT OF THE WILDERNESS 51
Not Perfect 53
Future 54
With me 55
Speak Lord 56
Words 57
JOY 58
Hear See Think! 59
Who Am I 60
Luggage 61
The Great Abide 62
I Submit 64
You Alone 65
My Life is in your hands 66
Let me not Forget 67
Breath of Life 68
Changed 69

CHAPTER 1

A JOURNEY WITH THE KING

WHY JESUS?

Why Jesus! I've tried him.
I took him at "his word" and found all he said to be true.
Although I may not understand it all,
I believe every word through and through!
I called to him and he answered me.
Delivered my soul and set me free.
He gave me a peace I had not known.
Restored my hope and allows me to carry on.
When I was sick and began to doubt. He drew close to me and helped me out.
He healed my body and my mind.
Touched my family, we are doing fine.
He does not dwell on sin. At the cross he dealt with them.
He sees me as his beloved child, his daughter, his princess, the apple of his eye.
He counted me worthy before my life began and it's because of him I am what I am.
Why Jesus?
He's the lover of my soul, the redeemer of sin.
He is the beginning and he is the end.
He is my healer, husband, deliverer, and friend!
He is hope for the hopeless.
The truth is in him.
Jesus is who he says he is!

MY IMMEASURABLE IMPOSSIBLE GOD

You can not be restrained by the shores of the oceans and sea Nor the measure of this world you've made in your glory and majesty What is impossible for you?
You do more than my eyes will ever see,
More than my ears can hear or my heart and mind comprehend

OH my immeasurable, impossible God

You stretched forth your hand into nothing and created everything You Oh God who hear the cry of your people and heal the brokenhearted and faint You who know the end from the beginning
who set all things in place

Oh my immeasurable, impossible God

What is impossible for you?, you know and see all
You who give and take away
You who build up and tear down
You who destroy and create
You who are able to open doors no man can touch
You who redeem our lives from despair
You who replace weeping with joy, and bondage for freedom and deliverance

You are my immeasurable, impossible God and nothing is impossible for you
So we look to you who can do all things
Who knew us before our time began
We look to you our immeasurable impossible God

But Jesus beheld [them], and said unto them, with men this is impossible; but with God all things are possible.

Matthew 19:26

WHO CAN COMPARE TO YOU

Who can compare to the Lord God Almighty
Creator of all things
Redeemer of mankind
Restorer of life Joy, Strength, peace!
Who can compare to you,
Who knows my every thought, and sees my every deed
Who knows the hairs on my head and can meet my every need
Who can compare to you
Who loves without limits, who pardons and judges
Who can compare to you

FATHER, SPIRIT, AND SON

I am Loved by the Father
I am cherished by the son
I am comforted by the Holy Spirit
They are three in one
In the Father power and strength
In the Son salvation and redemption
In the Spirit guidance and wisdom
In all three I live, move and have my being
I have the Father
I have the Son
I have the Holy Spirit
They are three in one

THE ONLY ONE

You are the only one who can crush and one come out better

The only one who can take but leave a place wealthier than before

Who can look at destruction but yet see construction

You are the only one who can add 2 +5 and have it equal a multitude

Who can have both the number two and the number three equal one

You are the only one who can speak what is not yet seen and have it already be

The only one who can speak and have it reach both past and present and last for eternity

Oh you are the only one by which men can cry out and be saved

Only you, you are the only one!

AMAZEMENT

You continue to amaze me oh God
Your love is simply amazing
I'm awestruck by your strength
With your love you keep drawing me closer and closer in
Sin no longer can entice, because your love is so inviting
You Oh Lord amaze me
You're my peace when things are crazy
Your voice calms the sea when troubled waters surround me
With one word you give me peace
Oh Lord you are so amazing
With you I never lack
When things begin to run out, you provide even that
Oh Lord you amaze me
When everyone else turns way
In your arms I always have a safe place
You Oh Lord amaze me
You understand every flaw
And create me anew when I call
You Oh Lord amaze me

When I want to walk away in whispers of love I can hear you say.... STAY
You Oh Lord amaze me
Every detail of my life matters to you
You have gone through hell and back so that I would know your love is true
You Oh lord amaze me
You have healed my every wound and care
I have no doubt that you are near
You oh Lord amaze me
In eternity I will one day behold your face
For you saved me with your amazing grace
You Oh Lord amaze me

THE GREAT EXCHANGE

As the dusk breaks to dawn and the night fades away so your love warms my heart and illuminates every place.
The darkness breaks, light appears
Joy replaces sorrow
Hope replaces despair
Rejoicing instead of weeping
Instead of turmoil peace is there
It's all exchanged in the glorious light of his love
Prosperity replaces my poverty
The living water quenches every thirst
I awake to find myself full, hunger is no more
Oh the glorious light of his love
In his presence there is an exchange and I am changed forever more

WHO IS GOD?

Who is God?
Has he changed?
Is he not able to deliver, heal, change, and restore
Has he gone back on his word and forsaken you Surely not!
He is God
He has not changed or forgotten you
He has heard your cries and seen your tears
Place your cares and eyes on him
He formed you with his hands You are a part of his master plan Who is God?
He is the redeemer, restorer, the one True God; He is strong and mighty, merciful on all he has made
He is Love He is God!

GRACE & MERCY

I'm astounded by your grace and mercy toward me
A sinner who doesn't deserve what you have for me
But you see through the sacrifice of Calvary and set me in heavenly places with thee.
You shower me with your love.
You uphold me with your mighty hand
You help me to live and walk according to your commands.

Even when we were dead in sins, hath quickened us together with Christ, (by grace ye are saved ;)But God, who is rich in mercy, for his great love wherewith he loved us, And hath raised [us] up together, and made [us] sit together in heavenly [places] in Christ Jesus:

Ephesians 2:4-6

THE REIGNING GIFT

He was born in a lonely manger,
a dusty, dirty stable
The smell of stench was all around but... .
He was God, royal and divine

The place where he came from was dim and grim.
Yet God chose this way for the redeemer of sin

The story that was told is true.
In many ways the incarnate Savior was a lot like you.
Born in filth, rebuked by men, persecuted for sin, betrayed by a friend

Yet his end was great as the story goes on
He offered love, forgiveness and in his death he atoned

So each day as we wake let us die to ourselves and extend to others the depth of the life he lived

May we offer the gift of forgiveness and peace and walk out the love that was birthed for you and me.

May we look to the heaven's an offer our praise The King born in a manger STILL REIGNS!

CHAPTER II

A WALK IN FAITH

FAITH VS. FACT

I hear the facts each day they scream
Disease runs in your family

But my faith screams back and with a shout: I am
healed and delivered disease and sickness is kicked out

I hear the facts each day they scream
you will never achieve your dreams

But faith shouts back, oh don't you know
I can do all things through Christ my Lord

Each day I hear the facts, they try to
rattle my mind

But faith says hold on, I am kept by the divine

I hear the facts it declares what's been broken can't be
repaired

Faith sighs; oh don't you see God's already began restoring me

I hear the facts they continually speak, you are alone and in misery

But faith says NO! He won't forsake me, He holds me in his arms and comforts me

Fact says you don't have enough

But faith says the earth is the Lord's and the fullness thereof

Fact says you serve a God you cannot see

Faith says, now we agree I serve a God I cannot see but it is by faith I believe and receive

MORE

There must be more than what we see
Beyond the satellites and galaxy
More to our existence, more than we can every know
More than joy, pain, sorrow and hope
There must be more or life is vain
In the struggle for wealth, prosperity and gain
The hope for happiness, wholeness and health
There must be more, I feel it within myself
So much unexplained, much we do not know
Even though glimpses are given through science, religion and more
Our intellect still does not explain what some refer to as the Big Bang.
The origin of man from other life; insane or extraordinary is the origin of human life?
Something within me screams, there is so much more we have not seen.
Diseases lie all around many without cures that have been found. Despair, outrage, poverty, and war, confusion, illusions, economic loss, Racial tensions of who should be America's boss.
Oh there must be more, much more than we can see We are limited by our visions of reality, as we look around Internally we silently scream, more!
There must be an eternal existence to life, so much more to you and I.

YET, THERE IS STILL MORE

I am not limited
From everlasting to everlasting I am God
Your resources may seem low
I have a never ending supply
The Earth is mine and the fullness thereof
All that you need is found in my love
I have not ceased to care for you, my child
The sun still shines and the rain still falls
I am STILL blessing the one that I have called
You are my beloved
I know you by name
I am not done, my favor hasn't ceased
There is still more to come
Come, seek me
Treasures hidden, promises to be claimed
Covenants are still being fulfilled
Which from the beginning of time I ordained
You have tasted only a little of all that's in store
Yet there is still more
My child rest in my hands, rest in my plan!

Dedicated to
Bishop Anthony Alfred and First Lady Renee Alfred

Healing Hurting Hearts Ministries
Annual Bishop's Banquet 2009

UNEMPLOYMENT

Unemployment has given me peace
Shown me my true source and my real need

Unemployment has helped me to embrace those I love
And to rely on the one above

Unemployment has
Help me enjoy the simple things in life and pushed me to pursue Christ

Unemployment has allowed me to see me for who I am
Not to be defined by a job, a status, or a man

Unemployment has help me see
Oh Lord your plan is best for me!

SOUGHT AND BLESSED

As I pursued a new job
I sought the Lord
"How may I bless you, with this extra time my God?"
I begin to pray
I began to read
I begin to sing Glory to the King

I gave my time voluntarily
Helping those who had a need
And as I sought to please the King
Who is the source of everything
Strange things began to happen you see As I sought to honor him in my waiting

My family has not missed a meal
God has paid every bill
I'm not boasting
Please hear me out
Jesus is real without a doubt
And if you'll yield
He'll help you out
My every need the Savior fulfilled
As I have sought to do his will

When times were hard and deadlines were near
I went to the Father saying" Lord, please hear"
He did more than hear, he began to pour out
Debt reduction, and help with bills
Checks in the mail and cash from friends

I stood in awe, watching him provide
I knew the blessings were from the giver of life

I am so thankful, no words can explain
What begins to happen when you call and believe in his name
So if like me you're experiencing loss
Call on the Savior and let him work it out.
Believe in his word and begin to obey and He will bless you as you seek his way.

> But seek ye first the kingdom of God,
> and his righteousness; and all these
> things shall be added unto you.
>
> Matthew 6:33

ALL I NEED

Lord that I might hear and understand
Open my ears to hear and my eyes to see you
May I see the plot of the enemy and resist
That he would flee from my presence
Show me clear direction
I seek not wealth, riches, or honor but you
You are All I Need

EXPECTATION

I believe you have more, though I have sorrow, it is outweighed by my joy

My spirit is expecting, my heart is reflecting
On all that you've done and all you're yet to do

Oh Lord all your promises are true

You cover me; you hide me with your wings

Your love is a banner over me

Your presence fills me

Your spirit guides me

Your word assures me

TIME TO DANCE

It's time to dance, cast off your restraints
Be bond no longer
The spirit of depression is broken
YOU ARE FREE!
Free to dance
Free to sing
Free to hear
Free to see
YOU ARE FREE!

Oh dance for deliverance has come
Strongholds have been broken
Oh dance my daughter, Oh dance my son
By the blood of the lamb you have overcome
Oh dance in me for I have set the captive free!

Psalms 30:11

You have turned for me my mourning into dancing; You have put off my sackcloth and clothed me with gladness,

CHAPTER III

AVENUES OF THE HEART

THE LOVE OF THE FATHER

Oh the love you must have for us your children, your people
Our obedience warms your heart and brings a smile to your face
Like the child of a loving parent, your eyes turn dark in sadness when we pull away
You long for your children who have gone astray
You cry tears of sorrow when we disobey
But lovingly you reach for us to wipe away the pain
Oh the love of the Father!

LOVE

Beautiful, bountiful, broken and blessed

Blissful, blind, joy, and stress

LOVE!

So simple, so complicated, so needed, so frustrating

LOVE!

It's calling, drawing, pulling, hauling

LOVE!

Respectful, restful, so delectable!

LOVE!

YOU

There is no one worth more than you

You are unique, exquisite and fair

No one can compare to your personal flair

Your fingerprint is all your own.

Your walk, your thoughts to you they belong

There are images that try to portray your worth

But your value was set before your birth

Wonderful in all you do, there is no one worth more than you

You are the one you should adore

Adore you, love you, and shout out loud

You are extraordinary!

Stand tall, stand proud!

WOMAN

Woven in the tapestry of God's design
Outstanding in stature, oh how divine
Made in his imagine you are truly unique
Awesomely empowered with inner strength
Needed on the earth
You are the one that God uses to bring things forth
You are woman, you are his
Healing belongs to you
Because he holds you so dear
Hold your head up high
God has heard your cry and your redemption draws nigh!
Women never forget that you are covered because you are mine.

THE CHILD'S KEEPER

In earthen vessels he placed a gift
Covered it with his love, his presence, his strength
He opened her womb and placed life inside
A little one for her to guide
Through her womb the child came
But it is by his hand it will be sustained
From infancy, adolescence, and more
A mother guides the child given form above
However, there comes a time when the child grows
And thinks it's learned all it needs to know
The heart of the mother begins to breaks
As the child shakes loose from the nest she made
The child begins to stretch it wings, to explore life and what it means
The direction that the child takes can bring joy or more heartache
It is then the mother sees
What once was given may not be the child's present need
Although it hurts and is hard to receive
She releases the child to the King of kings
He looks from heaven and sees her pain
And holds her as the transition reigns
Through whispers of love he begins to speak
I gave them to you to love but they are mine to keep!

SHE HAS EVERYTHING

She has everything
She has become new
The hand of the master has washed her through and through
The pain of her yesterday is today's praise
How God has brought and carried her she is truly amazed!

She has everything
Her heart is now whole
What was broken and shattered... .
The Lord has restored

She has everything
Beauty untold
She is as rare as a ruby and worth her weight in gold
A peculiar treasure she is in deed
Fearfully and wonderfully made is she

She has everything
Her mind is renewed
She no longer conforms to what she use too
Wisdom, understanding, and discernment are hers
She decrees and declares and sees things happen in the earth

She has everything she abounds in love
Jealousy and envy don't belong to her
She is gracious and kind, to all she meets
Especially to those who share her belief

She has worth beyond measure
Her life is a treasure
Her mind is free
And she walks with ease
She is a child of the King
She Has Everything

        Dedicated to the S.H.E. Conference 2010
           Resurrected Life Christian Center
                Clarksville, Tennessee
          Pastor Marvin and Judy Quarles

MARRIAGE LESSON

We are yours. The two have become one
Wrap us together; wrap us in your love

Teach us how to love
Although we think we know

We need your guidance to guide us as we grow
We need to know the way that you have for us

Teach us that to give is the greatest gift in love
Teach us to be patient each and every day

Teach us oh Lord not to insist on our own way

Teach us to forgive each time that we are wronged To not keep a record, but to forget and move on.

Teach us not to boast but willingly to yield, not just to each other
But that your will might be fulfilled

Teach us to cherish, each moment that we share

We will laugh and we will cry
Reassure us that you are there

Teach us oh Lord, in all we say and do, to hold on to each other and to love like you.

1 Corinthians 13:4-8

Love suffers long and is kind; love does not envy; love does not parade itself, is not puffed up; 5 does not behave rudely, does not seek its own, is not provoked, thinks no evil; 6 does not rejoice in iniquity, but rejoices in the truth; 7 bears all things, believes all things, hopes all things, endures all things.

8 Love never fails.

BATTLE OF THE HEART

A battle is raging
I sense it in the air
I feel it in the wind
There is a battle Raging
One I must fight
One we must win
Temptation is lurking at every turn
The enemy breeds suspension and distrust
Speak to the heart of my beloved
Give him the strength to resist
Give me the strength to love

I STILL HAVE MY SMILE!

If you know part of my story, then you know why
I still have my smile

Sickness came and tried to stay for a while
attacked my body and even my child
But, I still have my smile

Peace left my home
at times I was confused, afraid, broken and alone
But I still have my smile

Love ones came and went
I looked around an all my money was spent
But I still have my smile

Life has been up and life has been down
But the light of God's love I have found
And.... I still have my smile

DISTRESS

People pulling at me from every side
I really want to go somewhere and hide
Lots of faces, few calls
Who really wants to hear it all
Life's demands won't let go
And I am learning how to say no
My body's tired Lord I need some rest
Send peace oh Lord, in my distress
I close my eyes and wipe my tears
So grateful that I feel you near I will lie down and go to sleep
Oh Father I need you to keep me!

CALL AND RESPONSE

My hand reaches out to touch you
My voice cries to the heavenlies
My soul longs for you my Lord, my King
I feel you drawing near, closer and closer to me
I surrender as your love surrounds me
You reach out to me
You meet me at my place of distress
You call me higher, unto thyself
Into your blessed peace, you redeem me
My soul cries holy and worthy is the Lamb of God who comes to see about me.

MY REFUGE

Lord you are my refuge and my strength
Build me up
Let me stand for you and you alone
May my joy be full as I think of your goodness and your mercy
Come quickly my Lord and do not tarry
Save us from the snare of the enemy
Loose every evil thing that binds us
Make our home a sanctuary to all who enter
Bless us with your presence

The Lord is a refuge for the oppressed he will not forsake those that seek him

Psalms 9:9-10

BIRTHDAY POEM

Oh what a day
It's your day, the day you have made
Yet it's my day, the day of my birth
I will rejoice
I will sing
I will give thanks unto you my king
Nothing has happened that you did not see
Nothing will come that you can't handle for me
Oh this is my day, the day you've given me
I celebrate for all I have seen
So much more to come
I leap for joy
Eye has not seen nor has ear heard
Oh you have so much more for me my Lord
I am yours and you are mine
Today has been given to me, your divine design
Today is yours
Today is mine
I will rejoice
You have been so kind

RESIDUE

There is still residue
But don't go back
Let me cleanse you
You have come too far, don't go back
All things have become new
Let me clean up the residue

Therefore, if anyone [is] in Christ, [he is] a new creation; old things have passed away; behold, all things have become new. 2 Chr 5:17

CHAPTER IV

COMING OUT OF THE WILDERNESS

NOT PERFECT

Not Perfect, but chosen, and willing
I'm not perfect far from it you see
But I refuse to let what I am not, to keep me from all I am to be
Predestined before one of my days began
God called me forth and carved me with his hands
I've traveled some time from there to now
Often I wonder how I've made it so far
I am not perfect, this I know
And what I've accomplished
He allowed to be so
Sometimes I feel like giving up, because I haven't achieved what I deem as worth
He whispers to me and my heart responds and understands
He has chosen me and my willing heart is all he demands
Oh I am not perfect, this is for sure
But each day I draw closer to perfection in the Lord He has chosen me, and I am so blessed so a willing vessel I will be and nothing less
Not perfect, but chosen and willing

FUTURE

Our future lies in the balance
We weigh every choice, every direction

With one wrong move destiny is delayed
So we weigh and we weigh and we weigh

Every choice, every option, every move
Destiny lies ahead and it's waiting on me and you!

                    Luke 14:28

"For which of you, intending to build a tower, does not sit down first and count the cost, whether he has [enough] to finish [it]—

WITH ME

Lord let my heart be sound in your statues, that I may not be ashamed
Give me understanding
Look upon me and be merciful
Order my steps in your word
Let not iniquity have dominion over me
Make thy face to shine upon your servant
Teach me your statues oh Lord
Your commandments are my delight
I delight in your word, your truth
I delight in your liberty
Give me understanding that I may live
Hear me according to thy loving kindness
You, oh Lord, are near
Let my cry come before thee,
Let my supplication come before your ears
Deliver according to your word
For I know that I am not alone
You are with me my Lord

SPEAK LORD

Lord prepare my heart
Open my eyes
Speak to me
My strength and my redeemer,
Speak
Speak to my heart Oh lord
Remove all of my sins and iniquities
That I may forever thirst after thee
For you alone are worthy
I thank you
I exalt you
I lift you up
Word of God Speak!

WORDS

Your words can travel far beyond my voice.
They speak through the distance and fill the void.
They pierce the ears of the deaf and let them hear.
They open the eyes of the blind to see things clear.

Your words they travel beyond the page.
They erase the past and reveal brighter days.
They take the old and create anew.
They water the desert and reveal you.

It is the Spirit who gives life; the flesh profits nothing. The words that I speak to you are spirit, and [they] are life.

John 6:63

JOY

Everyday I stand more amazed at the beauty of your holiness.
Each morning I awake in awe of your great love.
I'm touched by your mercy, and your power.
I am blessed by your presence each and every hour.
Your love astounds me.
In your grace I abound, your blessings surround.
You pick me up when I fall down and lift me to higher ground
Oh my Lord and my God what joy have I found!

HEAR SEE THINK!

Open their eyes and let them see beauty.
Lives clouded by pain and misery.
Open their hearts and let them feel joy.
Overwhelmed by life's woes.
Open their ears and let them hear whispers of love.
Forsaken and seemingly forgotten but
valuable beyond measure.
Open their minds to embrace the truth.
Going through life is difficult without you.
Let them see, feel, hear and know you
are near and you love them so!

WHO AM I

Who am I, that you are mindful of me
That you would allow me to speak on your behalf
T o represent your name
Who Am I that you allow me to declare and decree and see it come to be
Who am I that your spirit allows me to touch the broken with your words and power and make them new.
Who am I Oh God, that I would be used so mightily by you
Who am I?
I am yours!

LUGGAGE

I came to my master my luggage in my hand.
I begin to empty them out as he gently reaches for them
One by one I try to give, but he requests them all
He died so that I might live
My total deliverance has already been bought.
He paid the price when he died upon the cross.

THE GREAT ABIDE

I am setting your feet on the high places
Hold fast to my teachings
Do not depart from my words
Do not detour
Hold fast to the truth

Freedom has come
Deliverance is now
Walk in the new place
I have set you apart

Get up, get up, get up
Awake from your sleep
Walk in boldness
Walk in truth
Walk in power
Abide in me

Do not become weary in doing well
I will reward the diligent seekers
Have not I made the crooked places straight
Have I not refreshed your spirit and restored your joy

I have been your provider and source
El shaddi I am he
And all sufficiency is in me

Abide in me
Rest in Me
Rely on Me
Be blessed in me

I SUBMIT

Though the storm is raging, your peace oh God is sustaining
Your presence calms, your faithfulness assures me
Though the wind may blow around, threatening with howling sounds
I take refuge in you
You are my strength and my strong tower
I run to you and I am safe
I look not for you in other places but listen closely to what you say
Oh Lord you who command the winds and the waves
They hear you and obey
My life is truly in your hands
I submit myself to your plan and my life into your loving hands.

Written Labor Day 2008 on the wake of Hurricane Gustav, coming through
LA

YOU ALONE

May I ever be reminded of your love and your grace toward me
Let me not forget all your benefits
When I was deep in sin, you rescued me
You pursued me with your love
Oh Lord let me not forget
Let me not forget the delivering power of your blood
The redeemer of my soul, you are
Oh Lord I glorify you
My heart cries out to you with thanksgiving
Let me not forget you Are my God
I will bless your name Oh God
Your mercy is new every morning
Your grace sufficient every moment
I run to you and I am safe
You are my strong tower
You are the lover of my soul
You are my life
You are my all
You Oh God who meets every need
Who hears every prayer
Who mends my broken heart and makes me whole
Let me not forget
You Alone Are God!

MY LIFE IS IN YOUR HANDS

Forgiving me for tying you down to my own plans

My life is in your hands

You are greater than the great,
Wiser than the wise

All knowing, all powerful

What you have done before, you can do again

I know that you may alter how, but you have the master plan

Let me trust you forever more

You who know so much more

For I know the thoughts that I think toward you, says the LORD, thoughts of peace and not of evil, to give you a future and a hope.

Jeremiah 29:**11**

LET ME NOT FORGET

May I ever be reminded of you love and grace toward me
Let me not forget all your benefits
That yet when I was deep in sin
You rescued me; you pursued me with your love
Oh Lord, let me not forget

Let me not forget the delivering power of your blood
The redeemer of my soul are you
Oh Lord I glorify you
My heart cries out to you with thanksgiving

You are my God
Let me not forget.

BREATH OF LIFE

The peace that overflows
May I dwell here forever laid before your throne.
Your river flows and refreshes,
Your fire burns within
My eyes are fixed upon you as you breathe life into me once again!

CHANGED

I am no longer the same
My life has been touched
Priorities rearranged

In my weakness I received strength
Broken and torn
Frail and stressed
Now I walk around blessed, blessed, blessed

The storms of life use to overwhelm
Now I look at them
And release them to him
My God and Savior can handle it all
He hears me an answers when I call

I am changed I've been made new
Your life can be changed too
Believe in your heart and confess his name
Jesus Christ was raised from the dead
He is the reason for all I have said

I'm changed, I'm changed I know it's true
Jesus can change your life too

Talicia L. Smith is a minister of the gospel, divine writer, and passionate worshiper. Through her travels as a military wife, God has used her in many capacities. It is her desire to see the body of Christ walking in fellowship with the Father, Son and Holy Spirit manifesting the glory of God in their daily lives, living in the peace, prosperity and liberty of God.

As you read her inspired writings you will be encouraged and your life will be forever changed by the power of the Holy Spirit.

She is the wife of Sean D. Smith and has two beautiful daughters.

The enclosed poems and inspirational writings were written as she looked to God through the various challenges, and joys of life. They are a compellation of cries, exhortations and praise to the most high God as she has learned, and continues to learn how to walk by faith and not by sight according to 2 Corinthians 5:7.

www.ingramcontent.com/pod-product-compliance
Lightning Source LLC
LaVergne TN
LVHW011740060526
838200LV00051B/3271